W9-CCQ-913

The Quick Proposal Workbook

How to produce better grant proposals

in 25 – 50% less time

by

Daniel Lynn Conrad

Public Management Institute

358 Brannan Street
San Francisco, California 94107
Phone: 415/896-1900

Prepared with the special assistance of:

Betsy Cagan
Mark Staebler
Paul Hennessey
V. Srikanth
Joan Boisclair
David G. Bauer
James Vaccaro

Production and Graphics: Joan S. Schneider

The Quick Proposal Workbook

ISBN   0-916664-38-4

Library of Congress Catalogue No. 80-84209

© 1980 Public Management Institute

Reproduction of forms and worksheets permitted for individual use if credit is given to the Public Management Institute. Systematic or large-scale reproduction or distribution of other parts of the Quick Proposal Workbook -- or inclusion of items in publications for sale -- permitted only with prior written permission.

TABLE OF CONTENTS

PREFACE

If you've bought this book you've got a good idea. You have a project for your organization that you need funded -- an idea that needs money in order for it to become a reality. The problem you face is how to get that money. You've realized that in order to attract funders you must approach them in an orderly, convincing fashion.

You need help in transforming your idea into a workable project proposal, complete with facts and figures. You know that your project will benefit your community, your clients, and perhaps society at large. But how do you convince funders of the potential of your idea?

You need to turn your idea into a concrete proposal. And this workbook will allow you to do just that. Follow the step-by-step instructions given here and you will accomplish two things:

- You will organize your own thinking into systematic components, each of which can be analyzed and defended on its own. You will order these components into a coherent total project on our Grants Blueprint ^{tm}, which will serve as an in-house reference throughout your project, giving specific objectives, dollar figures and time limits necessary to make your idea a reality.

- You will learn how to make your proposal a successful marketing tool. You will learn to take your project and rewrite it systematically in order to appeal to specific potential donors.

At this point, you may be saying to yourself, "Wait a minute! I'm not selling anything! I'm asking for money for a project that anybody can see is a positive contribution to society. I'm not an industrialist!"

But this way of thinking leads only to frustration and failure. Part of a successful proposal is the thinking that precedes the writing. The Quick Proposal Workbook will help you reorganize your thinking about the entire grants process, and then will help you put this new knowledge to work for you. The written proposal is only the final outcome of many steps.

1

This System Approach to grantmanship is a 12-step method encompassing all the important aspects of a successful grant solicitation. The twelve steps are:

(1) Implement a Grants Readiness System (which insures that all information about your project is organized and easily accessible).

(2) Build your "webbing" networks.

(3) Develop grant-winning ideas.

(4) Creatively cross-index your ideas.

(5) Examine possible budget strategies.

(6) Research the field and pinpoint your most likely grant prospects.

(7) Effectively manage your initial contact with a funding source.

(8) Review your information and determine proposal strategies.

(9) Write an individual, tailored proposal.

(10) Review and revise proposal.

(11) Deal with the decision effectively.

(12) Develop continued grant support.

The thrust of this system is on discovering, then acting on the needs and desires of a funding source--rather than the needs and desires of your organization. Grants success depends on systematically focusing not on what _you_ want, but on how your project fulfills the needs of the granting agencies.

When you adopt this Systems Approach, you will quickly find your old ideas about effective grantsmanship changing. This becomes clearer if you think of the 12 steps listed above as the 12 hours on the face of a clock:

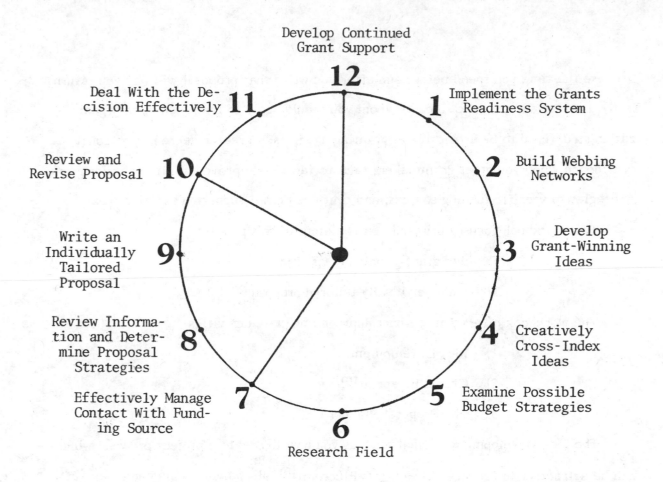

Develop Continued Grant Support — 12

Implement the Grants Readiness System — 1

Build Webbing Networks — 2

Develop Grant-Winning Ideas — 3

Creatively Cross-Index Ideas — 4

Examine Possible Budget Strategies — 5

Research Field — 6

Effectively Manage Contact With Funding Source — 7

Review Information and Determine Proposal Strategies — 8

Write an Individually Tailored Proposal — 9

Review and Revise Proposal — 10

Deal With the Decision Effectively — 11

Many grant seekers feel that the proposal is the most important aspect of their grant search. They spend more time writing it than they do on all other parts of the grants solicitation process—planning, research, personal contact, follow-up.

As the clock diagram illustrates, however, the proper emphasis for the grant seeker is on what comes before and after the preparation of the proposal. Proposal writing is only one "hour" in a system where every hour is important. Effective research, cultivation of funding sources, or a successful in-person contact with a funding official can do more to get you a grant than even the best proposal. In fact, you should spend at least 50% of your time and energy on the steps preparing you to write your grant request.

Needless to say, there's more work involved in the Systems Appraoch than in more traditional, proposal-oriented approaches to grantseeking. But the work will be worth it, because the time you spend before and after you write that proposal will pay you returns in the form of a more exact idea of whom you should apply to for funding; an organization structured to be attractive to granting agencies; a greater degree of personal confidence when you meet grantmakers face-to-face; an improved ability to tailor grant strategies to specific funding sources; and continued grant support, year after year.

This workbook focuses primarily on two steps of this process:

Develop grant-winning ideas; and

Write an individually tailored proposal.

The workbook offers a three-part approach to these activities:

1) Idea Development

2) Grants Blueprint^{tm}

3) The Proposal Planner

The Idea Development section teaches you how to create a project proposal which will be attractive to funders. The Grants Blueprint^{tm} allows you to plan and map out your entire project on a single sheet of paper. This blueprint provides a basis not only for writing a proposal and budget, but also for project management once your grant arrives.

The Proposal Planner helps you to take the idea you have developed in Part I, and the Grants Blueprint^{tm} you have produced in Part II, and create a well written, grant-winning proposal.

PART I: BEFORE YOU START WRITING:
IDEA DEVELOPMENT

WHERE TO START:

BASICS OF MARKETING FOR NONPROFITS

The first thing you have to do is abandon the old approaches to grantsmanship. To put it bluntly, it's important to stop selling your projects and begin marketing them.

What's the difference?

A slick salesman doesn't bother to find out what his potential customer wants, or what would be the best way to approach him/her. Instead, he just delivers his "pitch" and waits for a reaction. If the prospect buys, fine. If s/he doesn't, it's on to the next customer.

A good marketer, on the other hand, researches his market. He finds out who his potential customer is. He finds out what that customer wants. Only then does he design a product and sales approach tailored to that prospect.

In short, a salesman is most interested in selling, while a marketer is most concerned with customer satisfaction.

What is the point of all this for grant seekers?

Harry Woodward of the Chicago Foundation gives us a pretty good idea of the importance of marketing your project to a funding source when he says:

Keep in mind that the foundation or federal program has goals of its own. Thought should be given to how your program will further these goals. It is often wise to be specific. Too often, organizations appear to be concerned only with what the grant will do for them and not on what it could accomplish for those individuals and organizations contributing the money.

Put simply, most people looking for grant support adopt the role of salesman; they spend too much time thinking about their own needs and not enough time considering what their "customers" want. Their grant seeking process involves four steps:

1) Develop an idea for project.

2) Write a proposal.

3) Locate funding sources by word-of-mouth, previous grants experience, or in one or two directories.

4) Submit a proposal to those funding sources and wait for their decisions.

In short, they put all the emphasis on <u>their</u> needs, <u>their</u> project, <u>their</u> proposal. When it comes to locating and approaching a funding source, their "method" often deteriorates into trial and error. Then, like the slick salesman, they deliver the same "pitch" to each funding source. Little wonder many find their proposals in the return mail, rejected.

WHAT FUNDERS LOOK FOR

Once you have realized that you must market your project to potential funders, you realize that you must look at your organization, your project and your proposal <u>through the funders' eyes</u>. To make your proposal appealing you must write it in their terms, outlining goals and methods which the funders themselves would like to use.

You must evaluate your organization from the funder's viewpoint. Start now-- <u>before</u> you write a proposal. Begin to think in the funder's terms. The following criteria are used by one large corporation to make funding decisions. It may seem strange, but these questions, or others similar to them are asked by every funder, whether it is a corporation, foundation, or government agency.

1) In what ways will the donation benefit the funder?

2) If your project is to continue after the grant period, how do you plan to continue funding after the grant has run out?

3) Can you be specific about your organization's goals and objectives: what are they and how do they align with the funder's?

4) Who are your clients? Are they represented on your board? How do you integrate community members into your operations?

5) Is your operation cost efficient? What are the costs of funds raised?

6) How does your program enhance the funder's position in your community?

7) Exactly who are the people who oversee your operations (your Board of Directors and your project Advisory Board)?

8) How is your project original and effective? How can you show that you won't be duplicating the efforts of other agencies?

9) How can you show that your program will help to solve the problem it addresses?

The forms, worksheets and checklists in The Quick Proposal Workbook will help you to formulate clear answers to these questions among your staff, and to anticipate their being asked by a funder. The change in your thinking at this point will save you many hours of rewriting later.

BENEFITING THE FUNDER — AN ESSENTIAL
MARKETING CONCEPT FOR NONPROFITS

When you give a birthday or Christmas gift, you often expect a note of thanks. Sometimes you expect a gift in return, such as an invitation to dinner or flowers.

When funders support your project with money, they too expect a "thank you." This "thank you" is usually a feeling of altriusm, of having done something good for someone else. For your organization to relate most effectively with funders, you want to stress the benefits to the funder of your specific project.

The more successful you can make them feel, the better they like having funded your project. The more you publicize their help to you and your clients, the more likely you are to receive adequate current and future funding.

Here are seven ways to benefit a funder. You should try each of these techniques, and keep them in mind while preparing a proposal. Try to use several in every proposal.

1. **PROVIDE YOUR SERVICE CHEAPER** than other agencies offering similar programs. On pages 53 & 54 you will find a discussion and worksheet on cost-efficient program planning. You can show a funder -- using this worksheet -- that your "cost per client served" is lower and more efficient than other agencies' costs. So, you are showing the funder you are a better agency and deserve his money.

2. **PROVIDE A BETTER SERVICE.** If you can show that your program meets client needs better, you are showing the funder a better return on his investment. You may not be cheaper than similar agencies providing similar programs, but you can be better. Use our Uniqueness Chart (pp. 30-32), Program Profile Credibility Worksheet (p. 28), and letters of endorsement to offer proof to the funder that your service is better.

3. **GIVE THE FUNDER PUBLICITY: USE RECOGNITION TECHNIQUES.** Remember a funder is human and likes to have other people aware of his/her good deeds. The more aware you can make the community of the funder's contribution to your worthy project, the more likely it is that the funder will deal positively with your requests. Any well-run organization like yours will already have an on-going public relations campaign. Be sure that you include prominent mention of a funder's new gift in your regular

  - newsletters
  - press releases
  - public speeches to community groups
  - appearances on radio and TV.

Besides including your public thanks for funds received in your ongoing publicity programs, you should use the following special Recognition Techniques. Make sure that everyone is aware of your gratitude and of the great public service the funder has performed by:

- Having an <u>awards banquet,</u> and presenting the funder with a "Certificate of Merit." Make sure the media are invited.

- Having an engraved "Friends of Our Agency" plaque, and annually engrave it with the name of the donors who've given large amounts that year. Make sure the plaque is posted prominently in the entrance to your agency and that the funder sees it. (Send a photo!)

- Having an "Insiders' Circle" composed of funders and friends of your agency. Send them personal updates on your work and invite them quarterly to special dinners, cocktail hours, and other special events where they come to your premises to see your work. Make them feel that they are "a part of your family."

These and other techniques which you can devise are an integral part of securing continued funding. (Also see p. 78 for a fuller discussion of Dissemination).

5. <u>**REPORT REGULARLY TO THE FUNDER**</u>. Keep yourself in the funder's mind. Remind him/her of your positive contributions to the community and to society. An easy way to do this is to issue a newsletter, or a "Project Update." These can be cheaply produced and take a minimum amount of time, but they make a maximum effect on the funder. Make sure you mention that your work has been made possible by your funder in every issue. In addition, your director should send personal letters to a funding officer when personal contact has been established. These can be as simple and brief as a cover letter saying, "Dear Mary Sue, I thought you might like to know about our latest project milestone. The enclosed newsletter describes it, and I know it couldn't have happened without your help. Best, Steve."

6. <u>**HANDLE THE FUNDER'S MONEY WELL**</u>. Handling money well means both spending it wisely (planning an efficient and professional budget) and keeping good financial records. Hiring an independent accountant is a necessary investment that will return high dividends in credibility and accountability.

7. __THANK THE FUNDER OFTEN AND IN PUBLIC.__ Here's how to thank a funder and make him aware of your appreciation:

- Cite the funder's assistance in any printed material you produce. ("This project has been made possible by a grant from XYZ Corporation.")

- If building or improving facilities, make large signs which cite the funder's assistance, e.g. "The Joe Blow Gymnasium, made possible, in part, by The Mary Stevens Foundation."

- Any vehicles which your organization uses in connection with the funded program can have signs which mention the funder in the same way, e.g. "School Lunch-Mobile, provided with the help of the National Lumber Corporation."

- If you receive commendation from a professional or a civic organization, make sure your thanks to them for their recognition of you include a mention of the funder's assistance and your need for and appreciation of it.

These ways of "fluffing" funders, of making them feel good, all are proven methods of increasing the likelihood of a positive reception for future proposals.

THE SYSTEMS MODEL

AND PROPOSAL PLANNING

The best way to reorganize your conception of your program is a systematic one.
You should be able to verbalize and write down not only your goals, but your methods,
your objectives, and the ways you intend to evaluate them. We have found The Systems
Model an easy and effective way to visualize an organization's functions. It looks like
this:

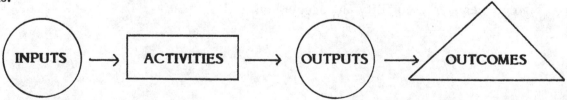

The **Inputs** to an organization are client and community needs. These needs start the
cycle which then develops:

The **Activities** to meet and solve these needs - the methodology, scheduling and

actual labor to implement your plans;

The **Outputs** of a nonprofit program, which are the products of its program efforts -

the short-term results of its activities.

The **Outcomes,** the most important part of the cycle (and often the most difficult to

assess): the <u>long-term</u> results of a program.

It helps to think of this Systems Model cycle in terms of an industry production

line. If we take an automobile assembly line, for instance, the model looks like this:

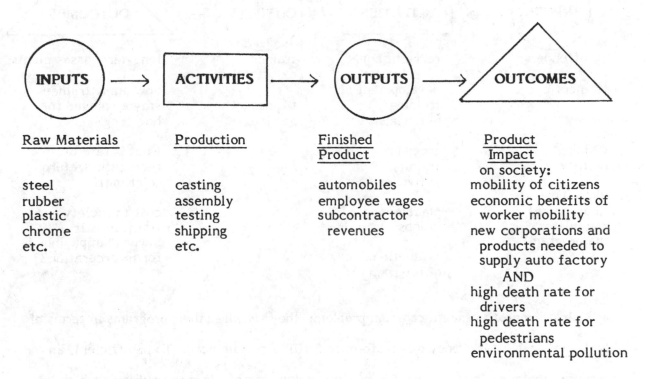

Raw Materials	Production	Finished Product	Product Impact on society:
steel	casting	automobiles	mobility of citizens
rubber	assembly	employee wages	economic benefits of
plastic	testing	subcontractor	worker mobility
chrome	shipping	revenues	new corporations and
etc.	etc.		products needed to
			supply auto factory
			AND
			high death rate for
			drivers
			high death rate for
			pedestrians
			environmental pollution

Here you can see that <u>outcomes</u> assume importance as the most far-reaching aspect

of the production cycle in the Systems Model. The benefits of auto production are

paralleled by detrimental effects which are often not recognized until they reach a

critical stage.

In addition, <u>outcomes</u> often spur a whole new cycle, by themselves being new

<u>inputs.</u> Continuing the example of automobile production, we can see that the negative

outcomes of high mortality rates and environmental pollution are problems in themselves. As problems for society they become new inputs, new challenges to society which must be recognized and solved.

To bring the Systems Model closer to home, let's use the example of a nonprofit organization dedicated to prisoner rehabilitation. The directors have thought of a program to train ex-offenders for employment in the home remodeling business. Here our Systems Model looks like this:

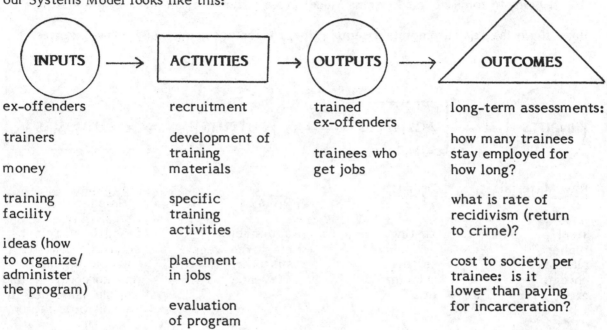

INPUTS	ACTIVITIES	OUTPUTS	OUTCOMES
ex-offenders	recruitment	trained ex-offenders	long-term assessments:
trainers	development of training		how many trainees stay employed for
money	materials	trainees who get jobs	how long?
training facility	specific training activities		what is rate of recidivism (return to crime)?
ideas (how to organize/ administer the program)	placement in jobs		cost to society per trainee: is it lower than paying for incarceration?
	evaluation of program		

Most nonprofits face a common problem: they visualize their programs in terms of activities: what tasks they can perform to fulfill a certain need. To be efficient, an organization must think in terms of outputs and outcomes. It is the outcome which interests the funder. Your organization's activities will be scrutinized only after the program outcome has been approved!

This distinction between activities, outputs, and outcomes leads us to a vital rule in constructing effective proposals:

```
┌─────────────────────────────────────────────────┐
│  START A PROPOSAL FROM PROGRAM OUTCOMES           │
│                                                   │
│  TO ATTRACT PROGRAM FUNDING.                      │
└─────────────────────────────────────────────────┘
```

Use the Systems Model in reverse to market your program. Start by describing the long-range benefits to society. This is what interests the funder. S/he is flooded with requests for money -- for inputs. Everyone needs money. This is an ordinary rule of life.

Your proposal must be extra-ordinary to attract attention and to win funding.

Remember, to construct your proposal, think through the Systems Model in reverse:

OUTCOMES		OUTPUTS		ACTIVITIES		INPUTS
Long Term Benefits to society	(from)	Achievement Of Visible Goals which provide gratification to the funder	(from)	Your Organi-zation's Program	(which sprang from)	Community/ Client Needs and your or-ganization's potential.

HOW TO DEVELOP AND MARKET FUNDABLE PROJECT IDEAS

At this point you may want to skip to the Proposal Writing section of this Workbook. After all, you probably have an idea in mind for a certain project or you wouldn't have turned for help in writing a proposal.

But wait. Read on and get the entire picture of pre-proposal planning and program design before you write the proposal. The idea you have in mind may not be the right one to submit at this time. If it is, you should have agreement from other people, both inside and outside your organization, on how to present your idea.

The Idea Development techniques presented here may not be used in writing the proposal you have in mind, but they should be used in your organization so you stockpile project ideas which can be developed almost immediately -- using the tools in this book -- when opportunities arise.

Take a pencil in hand and fill out the following "Problem/Need Analysis Worksheet" and "Idea Summary Worksheet." Copy the Worksheets and distribute them to appropriate staff members. The two Worksheets will give you an idea of what is fundable in your project, and what isn't; and they will give you records for future "Ideas That Got Away."

The "Problem/Need Analysis Worksheet" can serve as a rough outline which will help you fill in the "Idea Summary Worksheet". The Action, or Solution Suggested section of the "Idea Summary Worksheet" should reflect consideration of all aspects of your problem/need analysis.

PROBLEM/NEED ANALYSIS WORKSHEET

1. PROBLEM/NEED (list symptoms where appropriate)	2. Groups who have the Problem/Need
3. Related Problems/Needs	4. Secondary impact of the Problem/Need (groups affected)
5. Measures of the Problem/Need	6. Costs of the Problem/Need
7. Causes of the Problem/Need	8. What will happen if nothing is done about the Problem/Need
9. Why you and your organization are concerned with the Problem/Need	10. Community/Regional impact of the Problem/Need

© 1980 Public Management Institute

Date: _____   Writer: _____

IDEA SUMMARY WORKSEET

PROBLEM (Your assessment of the need or problem -- describe fully)

AFFECTS/SERVES (check as many client
types as applicable)

_____ men   _____ single
_____ women   _____ education level _____
_____ seniors   _____ income level _____
_____ Blacks   _____ foreign born
_____ Native Am.   _____ professionals
_____ Hispanic   _____ occupations _____
_____ other (_____)   _____ other specific groups:
_____ unemployed   _____
_____ handicapped   _____
_____ married   _____
_____ divorced

GEOGRAPHICAL AREAS IMPACTED (check or describe
                            where applicable)

City _____   State _____
Township _____   Fed. Region _____
County _____   Other Region _____
National _____   International _____

© 1980 Public Management Institute   (Cont'd.)

PRELIMINARY PROJECT TITLE (emphasize "solved problems")

ACTION

SOLUTION SUGGESTED (describe program, with special emphasis on methods)

IN PUT

PERSONNEL NEEDED TO IMPLEMENT SOLUTION (estimate)

approximate salary per week

1. Project Director _____ _____

2. Substitute/Alt. Director _____ _____

3. _____ _____

4. _____ _____

5. _____ _____

6. _____ _____

7. _____ _____

(list others on separate sheet as necessary)

   TOTAL PERSONNEL COST PER WEEK (add 1 - 7) _____

© 1980 Public Management Institute   (Cont'd.)

RESOURCES NEEDED TO IMPLEMENT SOLUTION

		check one:		Approx. Cost Per Week
		Own	Rent/Buy	

IN PUT

1. Equipment
   A. _____ ___ ___ $ _____
   B. _____ ___ ___ $ _____
   C. _____ ___ ___ $ _____
   D. _____ ___ ___ $ _____
   E. _____ ___ ___ $ _____
   F. _____ ___ ___ $ _____
2. Facilities
   A. _____ ___ ___ $ _____
   B. _____ ___ ___ $ _____
   C. _____ ___ ___ $ _____
3. Consultants;
   Contracted Services
   A. _____ ___ ___ $ _____
   B. _____ ___ ___ $ _____
   C. _____ ___ ___ $ _____
   D. _____ ___ ___ $ _____
   E. _____ ___ ___ $ _____
4. Travel Expenses
   A. _____ ___ ___ $ _____
   B. _____ ___ ___ $ _____
   C. _____ ___ ___ $ _____
5. Other
   A. _____ ___ ___ $ _____
   B. _____ ___ ___ $ _____

   Total $ _____

ESTIMATED LENGTH OF PROJECT _____ Weeks

ACTIVITIES

TOTAL ESTIMATED PROJECT COST

A. Total Estimated PERSONNEL (from above) _____

B. Total Estimated RESOURCES (from above) _____

C. Total Estimated Weekly Cost (add A plus B) _____

multiply by weeks in ESTIMATED
LENGTH OF PROJECT (from above) X _____ =

TOTAL ESTIMATED PROJECT COST _____

© 1980 Public Management Institute

(Cont'd.)

OBJECTIVES

List at least three specific outputs
you will achieve - give target date.

Target Date

OUT PUTS

1. _____   _____

2. _____   _____

3. _____   _____

4. _____   _____

5. _____   _____

LONG TERM BENEFITS TO SOCIETY

(What will project impact be one year after
project completion? After five years? After ten?)

OUT-COMES

MAJOR POSSIBLE PROBLEMS WITH PROJECT

1.

2.

3.

© 1980 Public Management Institute

HOW TO IMPROVE YOUR PROJECT IDEA:
6 WAYS TO MAKE A GOOD THING BETTER

Most of us are so proud of our having conceived a workable project idea that we react like a proud parent, and show our child around for approval from our friends. If we expect only praise and approval from staff, this is bad. If we hope for positive input and modification from criticism, then we are on the right track.

Process techniques give you ways to change the actual process by which you and your organization conceive ideas, encouraging a collective group process of suggestion and modification, and avoiding individual "entrepreneurial" thinking. We stress the need for group input on decisions because "two heads are better than one," and a single person's good idea can be made great if others can offer their perspective. Group processes offer benefits that single decision-making cannot.

Idea development is a creative process of review and adjustment. Where a logistical "nuts and bolts" decision often needs to be the responsibility of a single person (to be held accountable), a concept needs to be refined by many minds.

PROCESS TECHNIQUES: HOW TO DEVELOP FUNDABLE IDEAS

1. GIANT NOTEBOOK

A flipchart is a simple device which acts like a giant notebook or note pad. You attach large sheets of newsprint to a bulletin board in a prominent place in your meeting room, where everyone can see it. With a magic marker you write down each idea as it is presented.

The Giant Notebook technique is different from the average and usual group process. The typical group meeting is run by a leader, has a hierarchy of staff whose suggestions are valued in keeping with their positions of authority, and follows an agenda. Notes, if kept, are taken by a secretary who edits the proceedings.

A Giant Notebook session is one where all participants are forced to bring their ideas before the group. All ideas are written on the flipchart, and any comment, positive or negative, is forbidden until all possible suggestions on the topic have been written.

The reason for this process is that many good ideas are often squelched in typical meetings, because they are attacked immediately, without the benefit of perspective or synthesis. In a Giant Notebook session all ideas are noted and kept without immediate comment, since their value is not always immediately apparent.

In short, this is brainstorming with a flipchart.

2. A WISH LIST

A Wish List is simply a list of projects which staff members would like to see undertaken. It is composed of responses to the question, "If you had an unlimited amount of money to spend for the agency, what project would you create?"

The responses to the question encourage staff members to "think big." A common failing of nonprofits is that many workers are too used to "thinking small," to adopting the attitude of a beggar who is overjoyed at receiving crumbs. Funders are often attracted by innovative, bold thinking.

The Wish List helps all staffers see beyond immediate problems and goals and be prepared for -- and create -- new opportunities.

3. STORYBOARDS

A Storyboard provides a vehicle for an office meeting when meeting time is impossible. Often many staff persons are overworked and simply can't all be in the same place at the same time to share ideas.

A Storyboard is a metal bulletin board with magnets. On it is posted the "Problem of the Week," to which responses can be posted when people have the time. They can ponder the problem and submit ideas for group review at their convenience. This maximizes usage of individuals' time and minimizes overlap of ideas.

4. NOMINAL GROUP TECHNIQUE

Nominal Group Technique allows the benefits of a brainstorming session without the necessity for an individual to speak out in front of the group.

When the group leader poses the question to be solved and discussed, each group member writes on a sheet of paper his own answer to the problem. The papers are collected and then are submitted for group review and modification. This technique insures that (A) every group member participates, and (B) there is no fear of group criticism, since each suggestion may be kept confidential.

5. DELPHI TECHNIQUE

When the Greeks consulted the oracle at Delphi they hoped for answers to riddles. In grantsmanship, the Delphi Technique is an aid for those whose committee members are geographically spread out from one another, finding it difficult or expensive to meet in one place.

A questionnaire stating the project idea and its problems is sent to all members. The answers are summarized when received, and the results tabulated and used to formulate a new questionnaire. These comments and answers are in turn re-summarized and re-submitted to the group. In this way group input can refine a proposal idea without the group ever having to convene.

6. GET EXPERTS AS CONSULTANTS

Often your program's acceptance rests on its credibility. How can you show that your proposed project will actually perform the services you are forecasting? When you include expert outside help in the proposal conception process you are helping to insure your program's success. An outside advisor can often be the answer to the funder's question, "How do we know that this project will perform according to expectations?" The advisor provides assurance that your program will function correctly, if s/he has overseen similar programs in the past.

YOUR ASSETS AND HOW TO MARKET THEM

Once you have started to think in terms of marketing your proposal to funders, you will realize that much of making your program attractive lies in stressing your assets.

We all have assets and liabilities. This section tells you how to pinpoint and build your assets. Approach your funder with an imposing display of your strengths. Avoid discussion of your weaknesses.

We encourage you to think of your assets in three crucial areas:

- Credibility - prove that you will do what you say.

- Uniqueness - show what you can do that no one else does.

- Cost Effectiveness - show your funder that your service provides the best value for their dollars.

Turn the page and begin to rate your assets. When you understand your strengths you can present them forcefully to your funders.

ASSESSING AND DEVELOPING CREDIBILITY —

A PRE-PROPOSAL MARKETING "MUST"

Credibility derives from presenting a specific level of competence in your organization that will give funders the assurance that their dollars are well spent. You cannot just _claim_ that you will develop an effective program -- your proposal will be filed in the wastebasket. You need to show the funder how and why you are the best agency to deal with a pressing problem. Your agency, the problem it addressses, and your program all have to be credible.

There are four types of credibility, each of which present a set a questions you need to answer when you present your program to a funder.

1: **INSTITUTIONAL CREDIBILITY.** What is the track record of your institution and its past programs? Who funded them? Were they successful? What are the ongoing resources of your institution? Who are the staff members? What is their experience in the field?

2: **PROBLEM CREDIBILITY.** Is the proposed program actually addressing an obvious and pressing problem/need? What will be the project's impact on society? Is the problem obvious, tangible, and perceived as crucial by the community?

3: **PROGRAM CREDIBILITY.** Who are the persons to be involved in the program? What is their experience in the area? What kind of methodology does the proposal suggest? Has it been used successfully before? If not, what facts and figures support its adoption? Will this methodology be cost efficient?

4. **OUTSIDE CREDIBILITY.** Does the organization (and/or the program) have positive written endorsements from leaders in the field? Who are they? What do they say? Do the funders know them personally? What kind of Project Advisory Committee has been formed? Are the people on the committee knowledgeable? Will they actually oversee program operations?

5. **MARKETING CREDIBILITY.** Do project personnel communicate well to people both in and out of their field? Are the ideas behind your project presented clearly and provocatively? Do you have a plan to publicize your project? Do you have a plan to disseminate the results of your project?

NOTE: You must be aggressive when seeking endorsements. After someone has agreed to write a letter on your behalf, ask if you might submit a sample letter for his/her signature or rewriting. This does two things: it ensures timely cooperation (we all tend to put things off); and it ensures that s/he says the things about you that you need said. Often a lukewarm endorsement is negative, conveying the impression that nothing strongly positive can be said, that you are being "damned with faint praise."

An Advocate Network should be formed by a committee of your staff persons, using one of the Process Techniques for developing fundable ideas (pp. 22-24) to solicit a wide range of prospects. Then you should assign staff or volunteers to approach the prospects and secure their cooperation.

Use the following worksheet to rate your project's credibility. The input you receive from rating yourself can help you to formulate a convincing proposal.

CREDIBILITY WORKSHEET

PROJECT: _____   Date: _____

Writer: _____

Instructions:

Rate yourself 1 – 10 (10 is best) in each credibility area. If any item is less than seven, check in the appropriate column. Write in the name of the person responsible for constructing an Action Plan to remedy checked areas. Determine the due date of the Action Plan. Fill in the actual date of receipt of the plan.

	Credibility Area	Rate 1–10	Check if less than 7	Who is Responsible for constructing Action Plan to remedy?	Plan Due Date	Date Plan Received
Institution	1. Track record					
	2. Adequate institutional resources					
	3. Adequate long-range plan					
Problem/ Need	4. Pressing problem/need					
	5. Project impact on society					
Program	6. Personnel qualifications					
	7. Accepted approach to problem					
	8. Cost-efficient methods					
Outside Support	9. Endorsements					
	10. Advocate network					
	11. Project advisory committee					
Marketing Skills	12. Personal presentation skills					
	13. Proposal writing skills					
	14. Public relations skills					

© 1980 Public Management Institute

28

DETERMINING YOUR UNIQUE FEATURES

Suppose you walked into a job interview and were told: "This position requires someone with highly complex and specific skills; the work is vitally important to a great number of people and we can only have the best possible individual doing it. Can you tell me why you're the best?"

Do you know what you'd say?

In the highly conpetitive world of grants -- as in the tight job market -- you have to think best. Good and competent aren't enough. Many people are good and competent. You have to go further, determine what makes you unique in your field, what makes your organization or project the best.

The exercise on the next page has been designed to aid you in this process. It can be done either in a group meeting or through the mail (using the accompanying worksheet).

DETERMINING YOUR UNIQUE FEATURES: AN EXERCISE

Step 1. Have a meeting of your Board and staff. Have them "brainstorm" a complete list of responses for each of the four questions on this chart, which you should post on newsprint on the wall:

What makes us the best at what we do?	Why should a funding source give us money over another organization in our field?
What do we offer clients they can get nowhere else?	What do we offer funding sources they can get nowhere else?

Step 2. Make a master list of all answers.

Step 3. Give each person present 10 votes, to be distributed to the organization features s/he feels are most unique (you can give all 10 votes to one feature, or spread your votes out over many different ones).

Step 4. Tally the scores and pick the 5 highest scorers.

Step 5. Prepare a one-page description of each of these unique organization features. Describe in specific terms how and why you are unique. Quote endorsements. Cite statistics. Use comments of your clients. These sheets can now be used as the basis of your brochures, fund raising letters, and grant proposals. You can also use them to train people approaching funding sources for your organization; the one-page summaries will act as "scripts" for them.

Note: Steps 1, 2, and 3 can be done through the mail, or intra-agency memos, using the worksheets on pages 27 and 28.

© 1980 Public Management Institute

DETERMINING YOUR UNIQUE FEATURES: A WORKSHEET

WHAT MAKES US THE BEST AT WHAT WE DO?

#	Your Answers	Rating
1.		
2.		
3.		
4.		
5.		
6.		

WHY SHOULD A FUNDING SOURCE GIVE US MONEY OVER
ANOTHER ORGANIZATION IN OUR FIELD?

1.		
2.		
3.		
4.		
5.		
6.		

WHAT DO WE OFFER CLIENTS THEY CAN GET NOWHERE ELSE?

1.		
2.		
3.		
4.		
5.		
6.		

© 1980 Public Management Institute

DETERMINING YOUR UNIQUE FEATURES: A WORKSHEET (cont'd.)

WHAT DO WE OFFER FUNDING SOURCES THEY CAN GET NOWHERE ELSE?

#	Your Answers	Rating
1.		
2.		
3.		
4.		
5.		
6.		

© 1980 Public Management Institute

PROJECT BENEFITS WORKSHEET

Another method of determining your unique features is the Project Benefits Worksheet. It has been designed to help you translate basic information on your project into features and benefits that will appeal to funding officials.

In Column 1, note your answers to the <u>basic questions</u> about your work: The who, what, where, when, how and why of your organization.

Turn this data into <u>features</u> in Column 2. Features are your organization's strong points. . .central location, experienced staff, effective methods of helping your clients.

In Column 3, turn these features into benefits to your clients; in Column 4, turn them into benefits to your funders. Benefits are the <u>direct</u> advantages a client or funder receives as a result of your features. These might include an ease of client access or high quality of client service.

If any of these benefits are <u>unique</u>, check Column 5. These will be your strongest motivators when you approach funders for grants. Emphasize these benefits in your proposals and in-person contacts.

PROJECT BENEFITS WORKSHEET

Basic Questions	1 Answers	2 Features	3 Benefits to Clients	4 Benefits to Funders	5 Unique
WHAT					
WHERE					
WHO					
WHEN					
HOW					
WHY					

© 1980 Public Management Institute

PROJECT BENEFITS WORKSHEET: SAMPLE

Basic Questions	1 Answers	2 Features	3 Benefits to Clients	4 Benefits to Funders	5 Unique
WHAT	Nutrition Education Project	Only project of its kind in Mobile, Alabama	Offers unique services never before offered	Will serve as a model for future state wide, and possibly nation-wide programs	X
WHERE	Mobile, Alabama	State Capitol: will serve as a model for the South	Ease of client access	Visibility and importance of state control	X
WHO	Dr. Margaret Miller, Project Director	A leading nutritional educator and researcher, who has most recently served as a consultant to HEW	High quality of service	Improves credibility; less chance of failure	X
WHEN	Project to begin in 1981	Well-planned service	Greater chance of success	Assurance of well conceived project; less chance of failure	X
HOW	Through slide shows and educational publications	Informative and interesting presentation	Knowledge presented in an easily understandable manner	System transferable to other cities and states	X
WHY	To fill a pressing need: poor nutrition is growing among school aged children in Mobile at a rate of 15% per year.	Project specifically designed to meet the needs of the target population	Service provided for free and will be tailored to their needs by the initial survey results	High chance of project success	X

35

© 1980 Public Management Institute

Now that you have completed the Idea Development section of this Workbook, you are ready to consolidate your project plan into a single, detailed blueprint of action. The Grants Blueprint^{tm} provides you with a tool to demonstrate the clarity of your project plan, and to outline all the information about your project that you will need to detail in your grant proposal.

PART II: THE GRANTS BLUEPRINT^{tm}

THE GRANTS BLUEPRINT [tm]

A TOOL TO CONSTRUCT YOUR PROGRAM

While you are concerned with producing a convincing proposal, you must bear in mind that a proposal is only as good as the project it describes. An effective proposal describes an effective program. And an effective program must be thoroughly planned and mapped out. The Grants Blueprint [tm] helps you assemble all the data input for your program and to organize it in one place.

Once you have filled out a Grants Blueprint [tm] you are ready to write a convincing proposal.

The Grants Blueprint [tm] offers the following aids:

- it organizes your project

- it organizes your proposal

- it's useful in project management

- it makes budgeting easy

- it makes it easier to negotiate with funders

BECAUSE it organizes your data in one place for instant retrieval.

STEP I. <u>Fill in the OBJECTIVES blanks in Column A.</u> You may actually wish to start with a sheet of scratch paper in order to arrange your thinking into component objectives.

Many grant writers have difficulty writing objectives, generally because they find it hard to separate ends and means. Objectives are statements of end results, measurable statements of client benefits from your work. The statement, "To build a hospital wing" is, therefore, not a good objective. It is a <u>means</u> to an end, namely healthy people.

You can improve your ability to focus on end results by following this seven-step procedure for writing better objectives:

Step 1: <u>Determine Result Areas.</u>

Result areas are the key places you'll look to see improvement in your client population, (i.e., "Good Nutrition for the low income citizens of Mobile, Alabama").

Step 2: <u>Determine Measurement Indicators.</u>

Measurement Indicators are quantifiable parts of your result area. By measuring your performance with these indicators, you're able to see how well you are doing (i.e., knowledge as measured on standardized nutrition education).

Step 3: <u>Determine Performance Standards.</u>

Performance Standards answer the question, "How much (or little) of the measurement indicator do we need to consider ourselves successful?"

Example: "50% increase on the Nutrition Education Scale."

38

Step 4:   Determine the Time Frame.

The Time Frame is the amount of time in which you want to reach your performance standards. It's your deadline. You might, for example, decide you want to see a 50% increase on the Nutrition education scale by June 1, 1981.

Step 5:   Determine Cost Frames.

In other words, answer the question, "What is the maximum I want this to cost?" You might decide you don't want to spend more than $30,000 increasing nutritional education by March 1, 1981.

Step 6:   Write the Objectives.

This step combines the data you've generated in the previous five steps. The standard format for an objective is:

"To (action verb and statement reflecting your MEASUREMENT INDICATOR) by (PERFORMANCE STANDARD) by (DEADLINE) at a cost no more than (COST FRAME)." In our example, this would become:

"To increase the knowledge of low income food preparers in Mobile, Alabama by 50% on the Nutritional Education Scaly by March 1, 1981. at a cost of no more than $30,000."

Step 7:   Evaluate the Objective.

Review your objective, and answer the question, "Does this objective reflect the amount of change we want in the Result Area?" If your answer is "yes," you should have a workable objective. If not, chances are your Measurement Indicator is wrong, or your Performance Standards are too low. Go back to those steps and repeat the process.

You should evaluate your objectives against the "Criteria for Objectives" on page 44. You can also use "Writing Objectives: A Worksheet" on page 41, which gives you a standard form to use when going through this seven-step system.

Remember that Goals, Objectives and Methods are three distinct and different categories.

Goals are overall long-range agency purposes. They are necessary and compelling, but difficult to measure.

Objectives are specific, attainable, quantifiable components of a goal.

Methods are specific activities, action steps that you can use to achieve an objective.

Many persons find objectives more difficult to write than goals, because an objective has to be specific. An objective has four qualities:

1) it is specific: it tells exactly what kind or which problem is to be addressed;

2) it is measurable: it tells how much, how many, and how well the problem/need will be resolved;

3) it is time-bound: it gives a specific date for its own achievement;

4) it does not include the action steps and activities you will undertake to fulfill the objective. The activities are components which you will list and explain later.

WRITING OBJECTIVES: A WORKSHEET

1.	Result Areas (Insert one per box)		
2.	Measurement Indicators (Insert 1-3 per box - select the best one)		
3.	Performance Standards (for selected measure- ment indicators)		
4.	Do by (deadline)		
5.	Maximum cost		
6.	Finalized Objective (in form)		
7.	Evaluate - (does objective reflect the degree of change you hope in result area?)		

© 1981 Public Management Institute

WRITING OBJECTIVES: A SAMPLE WORKSHEET

1.	Result Areas (Insert one per box)	Low income food preparers in Mobile, Alabama	Preschool children in Mobile, Alabama
2.	Measurement Indicators (Insert 1-3 per box - select the best one)	Nutrition Education scale	Federal minimum daily requirements
3.	Performance Standards (for selected measure- ment indicators)	Increase by 50%	Increase to 75%
4.	Do by (deadline)	March 1, 1980	December 1, 1980
5.	Maximum cost	not to exceed $30,000	not to exceed $30,000
6.	Finalized Objective (in form)	To increase the knowledge of low-income food pre- parers in Mobile, Alabama by 50% on the Nutrition Education scale by 6/1/81 at a cost of no more than $30,000	To increase the daily vitamin intake of pre- school children in Mobile, Alabama to 75% of the Federal minimum daily requirements by 12/1/81 at a cost of no more than $30,000
7.	Evaluate - (does objective reflect the degree of change you hope in result area?)	YES	YES

© 1981 Public Management Institute

SAMPLE OBJECTIVES

EXAMPLES: OBJECTIVE	RIGHT	WRONG	CORRECTION
To reduce unemployment.		X	To reduce black teenage unemployment by 12% by June 1st, 1981, in the target area, for less than 100,000.
To improve maternal nutrition 22% by September 15, 1982.		X	To improve maternal nutrition by 22% on the Nutrition Measure-Measurement Scale among women aged 16 to 35 in Baltimore, Maryland by September, 1982 for less than $65,000
To provide 50% more additional shelf space in Civic Center Library by the end of the next academic year.	X		
Improve client attitude.		X	To raise client program ratings of "good" by 40% within two years of project start-up date, for less than $15,000

To summarize, Program Objectives should generally:

- Tell <u>who</u>

- Will do <u>what</u>

- <u>When</u>--

- For how <u>much</u>, and

- How this activity will be <u>measured and evaluated</u>.

CRITERIA FOR EVALUATING AN OBJECTIVE: A CHECKLIST

√	#	Criteria
	1.	It specifies a <u>result</u>, not an <u>activity</u>.
	2.	It describes just one result you want accomplished.
	3.	It starts with "to," followed by a verb.
	4.	It tells <u>when</u> the result is to be accomplished.
	5.	It emphasizes what will be done and when it will be done, but doesn't tell why or how it will be done.
	6.	It is feasible in light of projected resources available.
	7.	It is clearly related to one or more of the goals stated by the Board of Directors.
	8.	It is designed with, and understood by, those responsible for its implementation.
	9.	It is written on the basis of input from those to be affected by it (clients, community leaders, etc.).
	10.	It details cost parameters.
	11.	It is specific, measurable, and verifiable.
	12.	It allows for "flexibility" on the part of those carrying it out.
	13.	It is recorded in writing.

© 1980 Public Management Institute

STEP II.   <u>Fill in Column B, "Activities, Action Steps, Methods,"</u> with the appropriate

steps needed to accomplish each objective you listed in Column A.

This column may be the most difficult and crucial aspect of the Blueprint,

because here you are dissecting your objective, and determining the actual steps to

perform. Once you have listed every step necessary for an objective to be accom-

plished, it is a comparatively easy task to assign costs and time goals to them.

A NOTE ON PROCEDURE:

Fill in Columns A and B vertically first. Think of each vertical column as a

pie: it is something whole which you will cut into pieces.

Even after you have cut it into pieces, you still have a whole pie. In this way

you will have overlooked nothing.

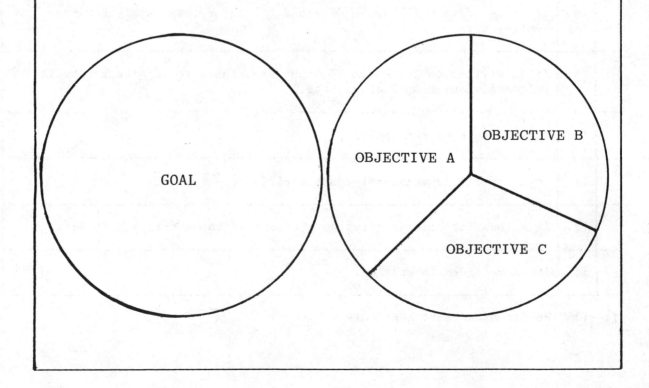

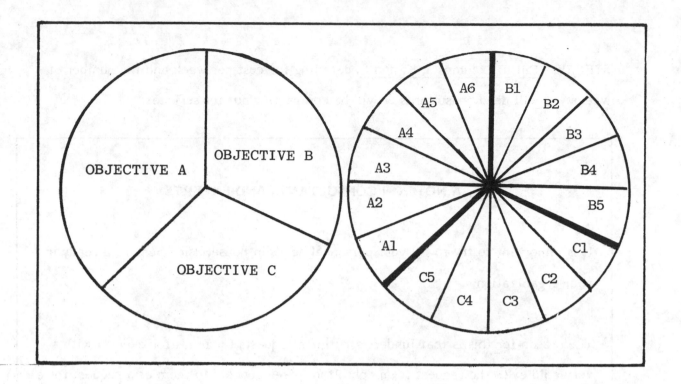

Remember: the point of being sure to fill in each column vertically first is to make sure that you have thought out each category in its entirety <u>before</u> completing the administrative details.

You will have wasted time if you have detailed several objectives, but overlapped or forgotten another.

Copy and fill in as many sheets of the Blueprint as necessary before beginning to complete columns C through S.

STEP III. <u>Fill in Columns C through I and Columns M through P</u>, giving for each Activity you detailed in Column B the appropriate

- time frame: columns C, D, and E;

- personnel: column F;

- cost for those personnel: columns G, H, and I;

- supplies, equipment and materials: columns M, N, O, and P.

STEP IV: <u>Fill in Columns J, K, and L,</u> detailing the cost per week and the number of weeks you will need consultants or will be contracting out for services.

A NOTE ON CONSULTANTS AND EXPERTS

It is important to try to fill your personnel needs in-house, using persons already in your organization.

The reason for this is that funders scrutinize requests for funds for experts with a very cold eye: the request for a consultant often appears to them as a request for a useless frill.

Also, they would prefer you to present yourselves as capable of solving the problem entirely from within your organization. They want to fund <u>you</u>, not others.

If you do need outside consultants, here are some practical methods to find reliable ones:

- Ask other nonprofits in your field whom they recommend.

- Ask funders whom they would recommend (be specific about the intended function they will fill).

- Ask consultants whom you've worked with before.

- Ask your local United Way (or any similar "umbrella" or areawide consolidated service agency).

- Ask your parent organization.

- Ask your local Foundation Center librarians.

- Ask other grantseekers in your field.

STEP V: Fill in Column Q, by adding the totals of columns I, L and P.

STEP VI: Finally, Fill in Columns R and S with Milestones of your progress, significant

components of the activities in Column B -- and fill in the date when you expect to

complete each Milestone.

These columns will help keep you abreast of what parts of your project have been

completed, and whether you are proceeding according to the schedule you laid out in

Columns C, D, and E.

THE GRANTS BLUEPRINT ™ © 19

DATE: June 15, 1980   PROJECT NAME: Nutrition Edu...

	OBJECTIVES (What are you going to accomplish?)	ACTIVITIES•ACTION STEPS•METHODS (How will you do it?)	DATE TO BEGIN	DATE TO END	WEEKS OR HOURS	WHO (will do it?)	PERSON... SALARIES & WAGES
	A	B	C	D	E	F	G
1	To increase the	A1. Pay rent	11/2/81	6/1/82			
2	knowledge of low	A2. Identify survey sample.	11/2	11/16	40	SD	360
3	income food preparers	+ print surveys (250)				Printer	
4	in Mobile, AL of	A3. Recruit 10 volunteers	11/9	11/23	.40	PD	400
5	nutritional content of	+ train for interviewing			10	SD	90
6	foods by 50% on the				35	AA	225
7	Nutrition Education				150	Vols/total	*(150)
8	scale by 6/1/81	A4. Conduct survey +	11/23	12/21	15	PD	150
9	at a cost of no more	analyze results			80	SD	720
10	than $30,000.				400	Vols/total	*(2000)
11					40	AA	260
12		A5. Design educational	12/21	2/1	160	PD	1600
13		program			80	AA	520
14		a. slide show			160	Photog.	
15		b. comic book			120	Writer	
16						Printer	
17						AV Lab	
18		A6. Implement educational	2/3	3/21	30	Photog.	
19		program			150	Vols/total	*(750)
20					100	PD	1000
21					120	AA	180
22		A7. Evaluation	4/28	6/1	80	PD	800
23					60	AA	390
24					80	SD	720
25	To increase the daily	B1. Pay rent	6/1	12/1			
26	vitamin intake of	B2. Pre test meals	6/1	6/15	40	SD	360
27	preschool children in				15	AA	98
28	Mobile, AL to 75%	B3. Conduct survey +	6/15	1/16	80	SD	720
29	of the Federal minimum	analyze results			50	AA	325
30	daily requirements by				100	Vols/total	*(500)
31	12/1/81 at a cost of	B4. Design training	7/19	8/16	160	PD	1600
32	no more than $30,000.	program			160	Photog.	
33					120	Writer	
34						Printer	
35						AV Lab	
36		B5. Implement training	8/16	10/10	30	Photog.	
37		program			150	PD	1500
38					80	AA	520
39					150	Vols/total	*(750)
40		B6. Evaluation	10/10	11/1	80	SD	720
41					120	PD	1200
42					120	AA	780

LIST KEY PERSONNEL / POSITION	% OF TIME ON PROJECT	SALARY/ WEEKS OR HOURS	NO. OF CLIENTS SERVED
Project Director	40	$10/hour	3000
Survey Director		$9/hour	
Administrative Assistant		$6.50/hour	COST PER CLIENT
Volunteers (10)		$5/hour	$12.82

COSTS REQUESTED FROM FUNDER ▶ 15,841

* DONATED COSTS ▶ 4,750

TOTAL COSTS ▶ 20,591

INDIRECT COSTS AVAILABLE UNDER

cation Project _____ **PROJECT DIRECTOR:** _Dr. Margaret Miller_

	PERSONNEL COSTS		CONSULTANTS • CONTRACT SERVICES			NON-PERSONNEL RESOURCES NEEDED SUPPLIES • EQUIPMENT • MATERIALS				SUB-TOTAL COST FOR ACTIVITY	MILESTONES PROGRESS INDICATOR		
FRINGE BENEFITS % OR $	TOTAL	WEEKS/HRS.	RATE	TOTAL	ITEM	COST/ITEM	QUANTITY	TOTAL COST	TOTAL OF I, L, P	ITEM	DATE	
H	**I**	**J**	**K**	**L**	**M**	**N**	**O**	**P**	**Q**	**R**	**S**	
					Office space	700/mo	6 mos	4200	4200			1
72	432				Office exp.	15/day 4 days	60		Survey printed	1/4	2
			3.5		Travel/local	.25/mi 75 mi	19	346	Sample chosen	1/16	3
80	480				Office exp.	15/day 10 days	150				4
18	108								Vols. trained	1/23	5
46	274										6
150	900								412			7
30	180				Travel/local	.25/mi 300 mi	75				8
144	864				Computer time		50		Survey completed	1/1	9
400	2400				Office exp.	15/day 20 days	300		Results analyzed	2/2	10
52	312								481			11
320	1920				Office exp.	15/day 25 days	375		Slide show comp.	1/29	12
104	624				Film	6/roll 30 rolls	180		Comic book	1/25	13
		4	700/wk	2800	Tapes	4/tape 2 tapes	8		Dates set	1/19	14
		3	500/wk	1500							15
			*(2315)								16
				180					9082			17
		.15	700/wk	525	Postage	.03/pc 2500 pc.	78		P.R. dist.	3/5	18
150	900				Slide scr. + proj.	50/day 10 days	*(500)		Slide shows	3/2	19
200	1200				Office exp.	15/day 20 days	300		Comics dist.	3/2	20
156	936				Travel/local	.25/mi 300 mi	75	4514			21
160	960				Computer time		50				22
78	468				Office exp.	15/day 25 days	375		Eval. report	6/1	23
144	864								2717			24
					Office space	700/mo 6 mos	4200	4200			25
72	432				Travel/local	.25/mi 5 mi	1		Test comp.	6/15	26
10	118				Office exp.	15/day 10 days	150	719			27
144	864				Office exp.	15/day 20 days	300		Survey comp.	7/2	28
65	390				Travel/local	.25/mi 200 mi	50		Results analyzed	7/16	29
100	600								2204			30
320	1920				Office exp.	15/day 20 days	300		Slideshow comp.	8/16	31
		4	700/wk	2800	Film	6/roll 30 rolls	180		Pamphlet	8/16	32
		4	500/wk		Tapes	4/tape 2 tapes	8		Dates set	7/26	33
			*(2000)						9388			34
		.15	700/wk	525	Postage	.03/pc 2500 pc.	78		PR dist.	8/16	35
300	1800				Slide scr. + proj	50/day 5 days	*(250)		Slide shows	10/16	36
104	624				Office exp.	15/day 20 days	300		Pamph. dist.	10/16	37
150	900				Travel/local	.25/mi 200 mi	50	4527			38
144	864				Office exp.	15/day 30 days	450		Eval. rept.	10/28	39
240	1440				Computer time		50				40
156	936				Travel/conference		425	4165	conference	11/1	41
											42
	19,010			10,545				2,855	42,410	81%		
	5,700			4,375				750	10,825	19%	◀	
	24,710			14,920				3,605	53,235	(T) 100%	◀	

◀ % OF TOTAL

THE GRANT ARE: _____ % TDC X BOX T _____ = _____ OR _____ % S&W X BOX U _____ = _____

PUBLIC MANAGEMENT INSTITUTE, 358 BRANNAN ST., SAN FRANCISCO, CA 94107 (415) 896-1900

______________ **PROJECT DIRECTOR:** ______________

NEL COSTS		CONSULTANTS • CONTRACT SERVICES			NON-PERSONNEL RESOURCES NEEDED SUPPLIES • EQUIPMENT • MATERIALS				SUB-TOTAL COST FOR ACTIVITY	MILESTONES PROGRESS INDICATOR		
RINGE NEFITS % OR $	TOTAL	WEEKS/HRS.	RATE	TOTAL	ITEM	COST/ITEM	QUANTITY	TOTAL COST	TOTAL OF I, L, P	ITEM	DATE	
H	I	J	K	L	M	N	O	P	Q	R	S	
												1
												2
												3
												4
												5
												6
												7
												8
												9
												10
												11
												12
												13
												14
												15
												16
												17
												18
												19
												20
												21
												22
												23
												24
												25
												26
												27
												28
												29
												30
												31
												32
												33
												34
												35
												36
												37
												38
												39
												40
												41
												42
										◀ % OF TOTAL		
										◀		
(U)									(T)	100% ◀		

THE GRANT ARE: _____% TDC X BOX T _____ = _____ OR _____% S&W X BOX U _____ = _____

THE GRANTS BLUEPRINT ™

c 198

DATE:_____   PROJECT NAME:_____

	OBJECTIVES (What are you going to accomplish?)	ACTIVITIES • ACTION STEPS • METHODS (How will you do it?)	DATE TO BEGIN	DATE TO END	WEEKS OR HOURS	WHO (will do it?)	PERSON SALARIES- & WAGES	
	A	B	C	D	E	F	G	
1								
2								
3								
4								
5								
6								
7								
8								
9								
10								
11								
12								
13								
14								
15								
16								
17								
18								
19								
20								
21								
22								
23								
24								
25								
26								
27								
28								
29								
30								
31								
32								
33								
34								
35								
36								
37								
38								
39								
40								
41								
42								

LIST KEY PERSONNEL POSITION	% OF TIME ON PROJECT	SALARY/ WEEKS OR HOURS	NO. OF CLIENTS SERVED	COSTS REQUESTED FROM FUNDER ▶	
				* DONATED COSTS ▶	
			COST PER CLIENT	TOTAL COSTS ▶	
				INDIRECT COSTS AVAILABLE UNDER	

THE GRANTS BLUEPRINT ^{tm} FORECASTER

The Grants Blueprint^{tm} Forecaster is an extension of the Blueprint itself, and is an aid to visualizing your project in its totality. Here you will transfer the information from Columns C, D, and E (the dates of each activity) and their total cost (from Column Q) and plot it in graphic form.

INSTRUCTIONS:

Number each activity/action step/method from the Grants Blueprint^{tm}, and place those numbers in the left hand column. On the light line next to each number draw a line representing the duration of time for each activity. On the dark line below write the dollar amount of this activity. Where the activity line crosses into more than one month, break down this figure into monthly figures (see sample).

Once all activities have been plotted, add up the figures for each quarter, or three months. This will allow you to break down your project expenses into quarterly amounts, and to plan when you will need large amounts of money a single time.

THE GRANTS BLUEPRINT FORECASTER™

©1980 PUBLIC MANAGEMENT INSTITUTE, 358 BRANNAN ST., SAN FRANCISCO, CA 94107, (415) 896-1900

ACTIV-ITY NO.	1	2	3	4	5	6	7	8	9	10	11	12	TOTAL COST FOR ACTIVITY
A1	700	700	700	700	700	700							4200
A2	546												546
A3	1912												1912
A4	800	3381											4181
A5		2100	7862										9962
A6				1600	2914								4514
A7						200	2517						2717
B1							700	700	700	700	700	700	4200
B2								719					719
B3								700	1504				2204
B4									2000	7388			9388
B5										527	3100	900	4527
B6												4165	4165

	1st QUARTER	2nd QUARTER	3rd QUARTER	4th QUARTER	TOTAL
	18701	6814	9540	18180	53235

QUARTERLY FORECAST OF EXPENDITURES ▲

THE GRANTS BLUEPRINT FORECASTER™

© PUBLIC MANAGEMENT INSTITUTE, 358 BRANNAN ST., SAN FRANCISCO, CA 94107, (415) 896-1900

ACTIV-ITY NO.	1	2	3	4	5	6	7	8	9	10	11	12	TOTAL COST FOR ACTIVITY

	1st QUARTER			2nd QUARTER			3rd QUARTER			4th QUARTER			TOTAL

QUARTERLY FORECAST OF EXPENDITURES ▲

COST/BENEFIT ANALYSIS WORKSHEET

An important aspect of almost any funded idea is its economic feasibility. Funding sources like to know you've chosen methods that will produce the best results for the least amount of money. This sheet will help you demonstrate this.

Fill in column A with brief descriptions of each method you are considering. Column B is for recording the price of each method to the funding agency (transfer from the bottom of Column Q on the Blue Print). Column C is for the number of persons served by this method. Column 4 is the cost per person (enter from bottom of columns on the Blueprint). Enter the respective advantages and disadvantages of each method in the next two columns. Then, compare the prices and advantages of each method. In Column G you should list any local organizations that duplicate your services, i.e., other organizations that deliver similar services to similar clients in your service area. Fill in the last column with your evaluation of the relative cost-efficiency of each one.

You should use this worksheet each time you begin refining your project ideas. You can also bring a completed "Cost/Benefit Analysis Worksheet" to preliminary meetings with funding officials. They will be impressed by the fact that you considered their financial interests while designing your project.

COST/BENEFIT ANALYSIS WORKSHEET

A Method	B Price	C # Of Persons	D Cost/ Person	E Advantages	F Disadvantages	G Duplication*	H Overall Evaluation

* List other organizations that deliver similar services.

© 1980 Public Management Institute

The completed Grants Blueprint[tm], Grants Blueprint Forecaster, and Cost Benefit Worksheet, provide you with the tools you need to create an organized, cohesive proposal, containing all information required by a funder.

PART III: THE PROPOSAL PLANNER

Some workspaces in The Proposal Planner may be irrelevant to your organization and project. If you find this to be the case, simply ignore them, and continue through the workbook.

CAUTION: When we talk about proposals, our rule is simple -- THE SHORTER THE BETTER. Don't be tempted to write a long proposal just because your Proposal Planner is filled with space for notes. On the contrary, you should edit as much as you can, and produce a concise, readable, and motivating proposal.

HOW TO USE THE PROPOSAL PLANNER

Now that you've gone through the process of Idea Development and looked at your proposal in terms of Marketing Your Assets, and have completed the Grants Blueprint,^{tm} you are ready to proceed to writing the proposal itself.

If you follow the instructions for the component parts of the proposal, filling in each blank as you go along, you will construct for yourself a viable written proposal that will be an integral part of your overall grants strategy.

The only aspect of the proposal that we can't lead you through is the concept of logical connection. You must make sure that the component sentences and paragraphs that you write have a logical flow -- that one part leads naturally to the ideas in the next. Only you can make sure that the reader will anticipate what's next in your narrative. You should you reread your entire proposal after you've written it, with logical continuity in mind, providing clear connections whenever they are absent.

Now, take a pencil and begin to write.

THE COVER LETTER

The cover letter is the personal aspect of an impersonal relationship. It is:

● <u>a social introduction</u>: it introduces you to the reader

● <u>a third party introduction</u>: you may introduce the read to the appropriate person from your staff who will be personally contacting the reader

● the <u>key to motivating the reader</u> to actually read your proposal: it must excite the reader by

   ● citing the urgency of the problem you will solve

   ● mentioning outstanding endorsements and community support for your project.

It also should:

● assure the funder that your Board has endorsed the proposal, since it should be signed by your Board's Chairperson, or highest officer involved in the project.

● briefly describe your project (in twenty-five words or less), but not take the place of the project summary (since the letter may become detached from the body of the proposal)

● end with a reminder that you expect to follow up the proposal with personal contact ("Looking forward to reviewing the proposal with you, I am . . . Yours sincerely . . ."), or will introduce the person who will contact the reader ("My associate, Miss Smith, will be speaking with you by the end of the month.")

● offer to provide more information and answer questions

● cite linkage persons (persons known to both your agency and to the funder) to supplement or establish personal relationships

● name the reference who referred you to the funder.

COVER LETTER

Points to cover:		Information on your project:
A.	Remind funding officials of previous contact with them; describe your project in one or two sentences (including funding desired)	
B.	Outline the need or define the problem as you see it; cite one or two supporting statistics	
C.	Briefly describe your solution to the problem (two to three sentences)	
D.	Present your credentials (have a top Officer or Board Chairperson sign the letter)	
E.	Other items	

© 1980 Public Management Institute

HOW TO WRITE A GOOD PROPOSAL TITLE

Many applicants give little thought to the title of their project. This is a mistake.

The title should be considered part of the <u>overall marketing concept</u> for your project. As such, remember that it should stress:

- <u>Outcomes</u> and <u>outputs</u> of your project (not inputs, the need for funds),

- <u>Client benefits</u> which come from your project, and

- <u>Societal benefits</u>: everyone will gain from the funder's contribution.

Most titles share several common problems:

1) They are wordy and prolix

2) They are too long

3) They are not understandable at first glance by the reader.

Avoid these pitfalls and make your title simple.

We can think of titles in two categories known to us all:

- The <u>newspaper story title</u> (a summary of the information presented following the title)

- The <u>magazine story title</u> (which <u>entices</u> by bending the information into somethig mysterious):

Newspaper: "Drug Deal Causes Death in Detroit"

vs.

Magazine: "What's Poisoning Detroit?"

You may, if you wish, make your title a combination of title and subtitle. With this combination, you may use the more enticing "magazine" kind of subtitle, as a catchy ending for a sober proposal title.

<u>Avoid</u>:

- <u>acronyms</u> (combinations of initials, like ASCAP - the American Society of Composers and Publishers)

- mythological and literary references - assume that your reader knows nothing, and don't make titles like "The Sisyphus Syndrome" or "Daniel Deronda's Devotion."

- being cute - leave alliteration and double entendre to political speechwriters and Time magazine.

- jargon and technical terms, unless your proposal is to be read by an expert in a specific field, who expects to be addressed in the terminology of his/her particular branch of expertise.

TITLE PAGE

Points to cover:	Information on your project:
A. your project title	
B. project duration	
C. amount requested	
D. your agency name, address, and phone	
E. your name, position, and phone	
F. date of application	

© 1980 Public Management Institute

HOW TO WRITE THE SUMMARY

The summary appears at the beginning of your proposal, but you should probably delay its writing until <u>after</u> you have completed the proposal. Then you yourself will have a clearer idea of exactly what is to be distilled and summarized.

If you choose to write it first, use the Project Idea Summary Worksheet, pp. 13-16.

If you write it last, use the information in the entire Proposal Planner section.

A good summary:

- identifies the applicant agency and establishes its credibility

- states the need or problem to be addressed

- outlines the objectives of the funding

- outlines the specific activities to meet these objectives

- gives dollar figures for the total project cost, and the percentage of funds already committed, with the amount asked for in the proposal.

Remember: **BE SPECIFIC, SIMPLE AND CLEAR.**

THE SUMMARY

Points to cover:		Information on your project:
A.	Summarize your request; include a one-figure cost estimate	
B.	Summarize the need as you see it (two sentences)	
C.	Summarize your objectives (two-three sentences)	
D.	Summarize your proposed methods (two-three sentences)	
E.	Summarize your evaluation design (how you plan to prove you've succeeded)	
F.	Briefly describe how your project relates to the granting agency's policies and interests	
G.	Summarize the benefits of your project to the funding agency (fulfillment of an announced funding program; satisfaction at helping solve a pressing local problem, etc.) Stress outcomes and outputs.	

© 1980 Public Management Institute

HOW TO WRITE THE INTRODUCTION

I. The introduction should:

- convince the reader that your agency has the background and capability to address the problem;

- interest him in finding out more--personally--about your work;

- interest and motivate him to read further through your proposal.

II. Remember:

- to use your agency letterhead stationery. It should have a list at one side or at the bottom of your board of directors. This immediately establishes credibility;

- to connect the paragraphs you write here in the Workbook in logical sequence; and

- to fill in the blanks below in the order in which they appear.

THE INTRODUCTION

Points to cover:		Information on your project:
A.	Describe who you are and what you do: how and why and when did you get started?	
B.	Outline your organization's goals (1 or 2 sentences). What have been your significant accomplishments to date?	
C.	Describe the relationship between this project and your organization's long-term goals.	
D.	Describe the academic and professional background of your staff; present the background and accomplishments of your project head.	
E.	Present your credentials: cite short commendations, quotes of well-known persons who have worked with you.	
F.	List your present sources of support and income: demonstrate that you have local support (money, facilities, donated services).	

Points to cover:		Information on your projects:
G.	Present other credibility builders: Are you a resource to others in the field? Is there an increasing need for your service? Is your service becoming more popular - is there a waiting list?	
H.	Describe your credentials <u>as they relate to this project:</u> what is your track record in this area? What facilities, staff do you have uniquely suited to this project?	

© 1980 Public Management Institute

HOW TO WRITE THE PROBLEM/NEED SECTION

As someone designing a program which will solve a problem, you may thing that the problem is so large and weighty that everyone must be able to see it as clearly as you do. This is rarely the case.

You must convince funders that a real need exists for your program.

The "Needs Assessment" or "Problem Statement" which you present is an integral part of your marketing strategy.

It should

- relate clearly to your organization's goals

- be demonstrated by credible statistics and quotations from authorities

- be a problem of soluble dimensions: you can't solve all the world's problems with one grant

- be stated in terms of outputs and outcomes, in terms of client needs and societal benefits.

Fill the following Problem/Need Statement by referring to the Problem/Need Analysis worksheet on page 16.

PROBLEM/NEED STATEMENT WORKSHEET

Points to cover:		Information on your project:
A.	Describe the need for this kind of project nationally or regionally	
B.	Outline the portion of this larger problem you plan to deal with	
C.	Supply statistical documentation of this specific or local problem (fewer statistics convincingly presented are better than many explained weakly)	
D.	Describe the need in the area your project will affect	
E.	State the need in terms of a single person ("Today the average income of a handicapped veteran is $4,500...")	
F.	Statements of community leaders • expert opinions (including quotations • government studies • survey results	
G.	Show this granting agency why it is the best source of support for this project (relate the problem/need to their interests)	

© 1980 Public Management Institute

HOW TO WRITE THE OBJECTIVES
AND METHODS SECTIONS:

In the Grants Blueprint^{tm} section of this workbook, you learned how to write objectives (see pp. 40-44). Your objectives should now be started as single sentences which specifically and quantifiably define the who, what, where, which, when, and how much aspects of your project goal. The objectives describe the end product, or desired situation which will derive from your project. They do not describe the process or the methods and activities that you will implement to achieve them. These methods and activities are described in separate section of your proposal.

The Methods Section should:

- describe <u>program activities</u> in detail: how do they fulfill objectives?

- describe <u>sequence, flow, and interrelationship</u> of activities

- describe planned <u>staffing of program</u>: who is responsible for what?

- describe clearly <u>client population</u> and method of determining client selection

- present a <u>reasonable scope</u> of activities which can be accomplished within the stated time frame and with the resources of your agency.

It should also:

- make reference to the <u>cost/benefit ratio</u> of your project

- should state <u>specific time frames</u>

- include a <u>discussion of risk</u> (why your success is probable)

- describe the <u>uniqueness</u> of your Methods and overall Project Design

- <u>assign responsibility</u> to specific individuals for each part of the project.

METHODS

Objectives (Statements)	Methods to Accomplish Objectives	Implementation (Sequence of Steps)

© 1980 Public Management Institute

METHODS: A CHECK LIST

HAVE I . . .	Yes	No	Your Remedy
1. summarized my approach in one or two sentences?			
2. related each method to a specific objective (possibly using a chart)?			
3. supported my choice of methods with references with results of cost/benefit analysis (see page 42)			
4. if methods are experimental, explained clearly why I chose them over others?			
5. broken my design into activities areas (e.g., planning, testing)? This makes the design easier to understand.			
6. established population or sample size sufficient to needs of project? (Check similar projects and discuss this key point with experts.)			
7. identified clearly who is in my population or sample?			

© 1980 Public Management Institute

HAVE I . . .	Yes	No	Your Remedy
8. explained how I chose them (e.g., randomly, based on need)?			
9. stated the future benefits of my project? (use data when appropriate.)			
10. stated clearly who will be responsible for which tasks?			
11. provided vitae for key project personnel? (include in appendix, and cite appendix in text.)			
12. explained the role of any consultant used?			
13. described how the project ties in with the normal workings of my organization or described how it is a separate entity?			
14. provided background information on any organization assisting me?			
15. obtained the letters of agreement from key personnel outside my organization? (these letters state the professional will work on the project, providing funding is received.)			

© Public Management Institute

HAVE I . . .	Yes	No	Your Remedy
16. made provision for potential personnel changes (indicating I have substitutes of equal stature ready)?			
17. explained the role of any advisory committees working on the project? (Give names and titles to add credibility.)			
18. described in necessary detail the facilities needed to carry out the project? (Emphasize what is already available, or what is being donated to the project.)			

© 1980 Public Management Institute

HOW TO WRITE THE EVALUATION SECTION

Evaluation is a key component of any program. It is extremely important to funders, since they want to be able to measure the progress your program has made and to determine whether their money was well spent.

Yet, many proposal writers neglect to construct an adequate evaluation component, feeling sure that the program will be a success merely because it is addressing a worthy problem.

Your evaluation section plan should make clear how you will measure:

- the extent to which your program has achieved its stated objectives

- the extent to which the attainment of these objectives can be directly attributable to your program (this relationship of cause and effect is a difficult one to establish)

- whether the program has been conducted in a manner consistent with your plan

It should include:

- names and credentials of evaluators, and their relationship (if any) to your organization

- Due dates of evaluation reports.

EVALUATION

Points to cover		Information on your project:
A.	Describe your <u>specific</u>, measurable criteria for success	
B.	Describe how you plan to collect data and monitor progress	
C.	Tell how you will keep records	
D.	Describe the evaluator • name and title credentials • objectivity (Is s/he an impartial third party?)	
E.	Outline your reporting procedures (how often you will report progress, format, and content of evaluation reports • give <u>specific</u> due dates	

© 1980 Public Management Institute

OTHER PROPOSAL COMPONENTS AND HOW TO WRITE THEM:

A. Future Funding

B. Dissemination

C. Appendix

A. FUTURE FUNDING

Few funders are interested in a project unless its program is self-sustaining. They have no desire to keep pouring money into a program, no matter how worthy it is, unless the need for continuing assistance has been made clear from the outset.

The following worksheet has been designed to help you make sure that your future funding needs are made clear and that your methods of meeting them align with the funder's interests.

FUTURE FUNDING

Points to cover:		Information on your project:
A.	Briefly outline your financing plan.	
B.	Describe your future budget needs for this project.	
C.	State why you cannot support project costs internally.	
D.	Mention other donors/funders involved in this project.	
E.	If government funding is unavailable, mention that fact. (Note: this is important in proposals to foundations and corporations.)	
F.	If you plan to ask for a renewal from this funding source, justify that request.	
G.	Describe your future funding plan. Include methods you will use to raise money for this project, and the amount to be raised with each method. (Suggested methods: membership fees; user charges; local organizations; other granting agencies; wealthy individuals; product sales.)	

© 1980 Public Management Institute

B. DISSEMINATION

To <u>disseminate</u> means to sow, or to spread around.

Your project actually has two purposes:

- Its stated purpose of solving the problem/need;

- to act as a <u>model</u> for similar charitable programs elsewhere which can help solve the same problem/need in their community.

Dissemination Is the Means With Which You

Let Others Know of Your Program and Your Methods

Here are some dissemination methods you should consider:

- a newsletter, interim reports, final report (journal articles)

- a workshop or conference on your project topic

- on-site visits by professional peers

- press releases, especially to professional publications

- papers presented to national or international conferences

- an audio-visual presentation

- briefings for government officials.

Remember to justify the budgeted costs of dissemination to the funder. Cite the advantages:

- increasing public awareness of your program

- soliciting additional support

- locating more clients

- alerting others in your field to new ideas.

Hopefully, your program of publicity and public relations will also be letting others know of your success, and of the altriusm and achievement of your staff! But that is a side benefit. The more publicity you get, the more credentials you attain--which in turn will help generate funding for future projects and for your agency's growth. Be sure to keep all clippings, papers, reports and announcements as aids in your credibility program.

Give careful thought to constructing a coordinated publicity program. Delegate authority to one person to write press releases, attend conferences, and so on.

In this section of your proposal, summarize your plan in order to let funders know that you consider the sharing of information to be an integral part of the project.

DISSEMINATION

Points to cover:		Information on your project:
A.	Describe your proposed method of disseminating project information (papers, reports, conferences, etc.).	
B.	Describe groups who should get information on your project (colleagues, general public, potential clients).	
C.	Explain why it is important to reach them (locate clients, raise money, help others start similar projects).	
D.	Person in charge of dissemination.	

© 1980 Public Management Institute

C. THE APPENDIX

If you or anyone you know has ever had surgery for removal of his appendix, then you know that an often forgotten and neglected organ can prove quite important.

So it is with the appendix to your proposal. It contains vital information which some people tend to forget. It is "last, but not least" in your proposal.

The following sheet includes vital points to cover in your appendix. If your proposal includes references to these supporting documents in your text, you should refer in your narrative to the exact page in the appendix to which the reader should turn.

Pages of an appendix are numbered sequentially with the body of the text.

Each item on the following worksheet would be a separate, lettered Appendix, e.g., "Appendix A, List of Board Members," "Appendix B, Staff Vitae," and so on.

The plural of "Appendix" is "Apendices."

APPENDIX

Points to Cover:		Information on your project:
A.	endorsement letters, certifications	
B.	list of board members and officers with titles	
C.	vitae of key personnel	
D.	tables; graphs; statistics supporting need, successes and past performances	
E.	publications, publicity	

© 1980 Public Management Institute   (Cont'd.)

Points to Cover:	Information on your project:
F. donors/supporters	
G. other funding sources you are submitting proposal to	

© 1980 Public Management Institute

BUDGET PREPARATION WORKBOOK

The budget may be the key to your proposal. After all, you <u>are</u> asking for money, and your budget is the concrete way you show you need it.

Filling in the Grants Blueprint^{tm} led you to prepare a budget by each activity to be accomplished in your project.

The Budget Preparation Workbook will serve as a bridge between the Grants Blueprint^{tm} and your final budget to be presented to a funder.

The worksheets that comprise the Budget Preparation workbook should be filled out in as much detail as possible. Then, tally your figures into the final format shown in the Sample Budget, pp. 96 through 98.

Do not forget to check your arithmetic. Your funders will check it for you.

As you fill in your Budget Preparation Workbook, keep these things in mind:

- <u>Every project is different.</u> Space has been provided for items not included in the Workbook that are part of your project cost.

- <u>Make sure you total the "requested" and "donated" columns.</u> This allows your planners to see how much volunteer time and donated budget items are committed to each organization program.

- <u>If you are in doubt about a budget figure, get expert input:</u> Call a fellow staff member, or get in touch with another organization that has conducted a similar project.

Finally, keep copies of all your budgets. They are useful in putting together future budgets, and also help you keep track of changing costs over the years.

A NOTE ON BUDGETING INDIRECT COSTS

Many grant seeking organizations include a budget line called "indirect costs" in their proposals. This budget item covers all costs not directly related to the project; it represents the organization overhead associated with the performance of your grant project.

An indirect cost rate is usually expressed in budgets as a percentage of one of either: salaries plus wages excluding fringe benefits ("S&W"); or total direct costs (TDC).

You will need to negotiate an indirect cost rate with each foundation or corporation you approach. Many do not allow indirect costs in budgets they fund. It is therefore important to have a clear understanding of a funder's indirect costs policy before submitting a budgeted proposal.

Many larger institutions negotiate with the federal government to get a standard indirect cost rate they can use in all proposals they submit to funding agencies. If you are interested in negotiating such a rate, get in touch with the Regional Comptroller of the Federal region in which you reside.

COST SUMMARY — PERSONNEL

(to be completed by program directors
in conjunction with supervisors)

1. This form consists of two pages, one for "Salaries, Wages and Fringe Benefits," the other for "Consultants/Contract Services".

2. On both pages, compute the cost totals at the bottom of the page.

3. These figures can be derived from columns E through L on your Grants Blueprint.

4. Round all figures to the nearest dollar.

COST SUMMARY: PERSONNEL

Salaries, Wages and Fringe Benefits

Program Name _____   Program Director _____   By _____

Person	Time	Pay Rate	Gross Pay	Fringe Benefits	Total
Totals					

© 1980 Public Management Institute

COST SUMMARY: PERSONNEL

Consultants/Contract Services

Program Name _____ Program Director _____ By _____

Name/Title	Time	Cost
Total		

© 1980 Public Management Institute

COST SUMMARY — NON PERSONNEL

(To be completed by program directors
in conjunction with supervisors)

1. This form consists of five pages, each page containing two items:

    Page 1 - Rent and Maintenance

    Page 2 - Utilities and Insurance

    Page 3 - Travel Out of Town and Local

    Page 4 - Depreciation and Office Supplies/Expenses

    Page 5 - Telephone and Other

2. On each page, compute the cost totals for each item.

3. These figures can be derived from columns M through Q of your
    Grants Blueprint.

4. Round all figures to the nearest dollar.

Program Name: _____   Program Director: _____   By: _____

Rent	Detail	Amount
	TOTAL:	

Maintenance	Detail	Amount
	TOTAL:	

© 1980 Public Management Institute

COST SUMMARY: NON-PERSONNEL   UTILITIES AND INSURANCE   Page ___ of ___

Program Name: _____   Program Director: _____   By: _____

Utilities	Detail	Amount
	TOTAL:	

Insurance	Detail	Amount
	TOTAL:	

91

© 1980 Public Management Institute

Program Name: _____   Program Director: _____   By: _____

Travel Out-of-Town	Detail	Amount
	TOTAL:	

Travel/Local	Detail	Amount
	TOTAL:	

© 1980 Public Management Institute

COST SUMMARY: NON-PERSONNEL   DEPRECIATION AND OFFICE EXPENSES   Page ___ of ___

Program Name: _____   Program Director: _____   By: _____

Depreciation	Detail	Amount
	TOTAL:	

Office Supplies and Expenses	Detail	Amount
	TOTAL:	

© 1980 Public Management Institute

COST SUMMARY: NON-PERSONNEL   **TELEPHONE AND OTHER**   Page ___ of ___

Program Name: _____   Program Director: _____   By: _____

	Detail	Amount
Telephone		
	TOTAL:	

	Detail	Amount
Other		
	TOTAL:	

© 1980 Public Management Institute

94

A SAMPLE PROJECT BUDGET

A SAMPLE PROJECT BUDGET

Project: Nutrition Education	Expen-diture Total	Donated/ In Kind	Requested From This Source
	$53,235	$10,825	$42,410
I. Personnel			
A. _Salaries, Wages_			
Project Director @ $20,625 per year x 1 yr. x 40% time	8,250		8,250
Survey Director @ $18,450 per year x 1 yr. x 20% time	3,690		3,690
Admin. Asst. @ $13,005 per year x 1 yr. x 30% time	3,901		3,901
10 Volunteers @ $9,500 per year x 1 yr. x 5% time	4,750	4,750	
B. _Fringe Benefits_			
(20% of Salaries & Wages)			
Project Director	1,650		1,650
Survey Director	738		738
Administrative Asst.	781		781
C. _Consultants/Contracted Services_			
Media/slide show producers			
9.5 wks. @ $700/wk.	6,650		6,650
Writer			
7 wks. @ $500/wk.	3,500		3,500
Printer			
Surveys	35		35
Printer			
Comic book	2,375	2,375	
Pamphlet	2,000	2,000	
A/V Lab:			
2 ten minute slide shows @ $180 each	360		360
PERSONNEL SUBTOTAL	$39,360	$10,075	$29,555

© 1980 Public Management Institute

(Cont'd.)

A SAMPLE PROJECT BUDGET (Cont'd.)

Project: Nutrition Education	Expen-diture Total	Donated/ In Kind	Requested From This Source
	$53,235	$10,825	$42,410
II. Non-Personnel			
A. Office Space Rent & Utilities[1] ($700 x 12 mos)	$8,400		$8,400
B. Equipment & Supplies Office Expenses/Supplies[2] ($15/day for 204 days)	3,060		3,060
C. Travel Local Project Dir. (300 miles @ .25/mi.)	75		75
Survey Dir. (332 miles @ .25/mi.)	83		83
Volunteers (520 miles @ .25/mi.)	130		130
Out-of-town Project Director to American Institute of Nutrition Conference 11/1 - 11/3, 1981 in St. Louis[3] (1 round trip economy airfare @ $200, plus per diem expenses @ $75/day x 3 days)	425		425

Notes:

[1] The Nutrition Alliance, our parent organization, will rent our project space in their office. Utilities will be included in the $700/mo. rent.

[2] The Nutrition Alliance will offer our project all office supplies, office furniture and telephone expenses at a cost of $15/day.

[3] Project Director will be keynote speaker at the National conference of the American Institute on Nutrition. She will speak on the subject of "Educating Minority Families About Nutrition.

© 1980 Public Management Institute

(Cont'd.)

A SAMPLE PROJECT BUDGET (Cont'd.)

Project: Nutrition Education	Expen- diture Total	Donated/ In Kind	Requested From This Source
	$53,235	$10,825	$42,410

D. <u>Other Non-Personnel costs</u>
 	
  Computer time to analyze survey data
    (3 rental times @ $50 per usage)
  Slide screen and projector rental
    (15 days @ $50/day)
  Film 660 rolls @ $6/roll
  Tapes (4 tapes @ $41/tape)
  Postage (5,000 pieces @ .031/pc.)
	
	150
	
	750
	360
	16
	156
		
		750
			
			150
			
			360
			16
			156

SUBTOTAL NON-PERSONNEL	$13,605	$750	$12,855
SUBTOTAL PERSONNEL	$39,630	$10,075	$29,555
PROJECT TOTAL	$53,235	$10,825	$42,410
PERCENTAGE	100%	19%	81%

© 1980 Public Management Institute

PART IV:

POST-PROPOSAL EVALUATION AND

REVIEW TECHNIQUES

EFFECTIVE COMMUNICATION: PROSE STYLE

Often <u>how</u> we say something is as important as what we're saying. Keep in mind the following tips to guide you writing style as you prepare and revise your proposal:

- Write short sentences when possible.

- Vary sentence length within paragraphs to avoid monotony.

- Never use a big word when a smaller word will do.

- Leave bureaucratese to the bureaucrats.

CAN YOU <u>OUTLINE</u> YOUR PROPOSAL FROM START TO FINISH?

CAN YOU OUTLINE EACH SECTION?

DOES THE FIRST SENTENCE OF EACH PARAGRAPH INTRODUCE THE MAIN IDEA?

IF YOU TOOK THE FIRST SENTENCE OF EACH PARAGRAPH IN SEQUENCE, WOULD THE RESULTING PARAGRAPH MAKE SENSE? (This emphasizes logical continuity.)

- Who is going to be reading the proposal? Did you write it expressly for that reader? (Ask for samples of proposals that have already been accepted to get an idea of what appeals.)

- Is your proposal as short as possible? (Effective length is usually under ten pages.)

- REMEMBER: Make it simple. Make it clear. Make it logical. Have someone from outside your office and outside your field read your proposal. Can s/he understand it?

EFFECTIVE COMMUNICATION: VISUAL APPEARANCE

The visual physical aspect of your proposal is an important aid in convincing a funder to actually read your proposal.

If you squish all your sentences together like this without double spacing, or if you make the whole page appear one dark black blue it makes it appear uninviting. So who wants to read it?

VARY THE APPEARANCE OF THE PRINTED PAGE

- **by using boldface type;**

- by using subheadings and <u>underlines</u> to emphasize logical divisions;

- by using arrows, charts and indentations;

- by using "bullets" like these (just type a lower case o and pencil it in);

- remember that you are <u>selling</u> your project, and making your proposal attractive is an essential ingredient for a sale.

Don't be afraid to use paper! Double space whenever you can. Quadruple space to isolate important paragraphs.

On the other hand, avoid colored paper, fancy typefaces, glossy covers and fancy binders. These gimmicks all convince a funder that you waste money on frills.

You want to appear sober and responsible, while presenting an attractive and readable proposal.

46 TIPS ON HOW TO WRITE GRANT PROPOSALS

PROCEDURE

1. Personalize and tailor your proposals to individual funders.

2. Know as much as you can about your funder before starting to write your proposal.

3. Talk to other grantees about their proposals to a funder before writing yours. Ask about the funder's preferences in:

    - length
    - complexity
    - budget detail
    - statistical support
    - personal contact before proposal submission

    Write your proposal accordingly.

4. Get you project idea critiqued by a number of associates before writing a full-scale proposal. Use the Idea Summary Forms, pp. 17 through 20.

5. Don't use a committee.

    - The fewer writers involved, the better the proposal.
    - Preferably, the project innovator should be the author, with editorial assistance by a grants coordinator.

6. Don't finalize your budget until you discuss it with the funder. (Ask "We are thinking of requesting $_____. Is that appropriate?")

7. Write your budget first. Then make sure your proposal supports each item in that budget.

8. Write your summary last, after you have finished the major parts of your application.

9. Don't try for perfection on your first draft. Get down your ideas, then edit and rewrite.

10. Use a proposal review committee to give you input on strengths and weaknesses of your proposal.

11. Have an associate or friend not directly involved in your project proofread your proposal, looking for:

    - grammatical mistakes
    - logical inconsistencies
    - unjustified budget items
    - undefined or confusing terms
    - unsupported arguments, unfounded assumptions, weak documentation
    - ways to improve overall proposal impact

CONTENT

1. If the proposal is a long one (of 10 pages or more), prepare a table of contents.

2. Don't make a mystery out of your proposal. Start right in the with the most important point.

3. Use models (a model for a three-step program could be a triangle, each corner representing a step, each side representing the relationship between the steps).

4. Use graphs, charts, and maps to illustrate your points whenever possible.

5. Use captioned photographs.

6. Use one or two clear statistics rather than a number of ineffective ones.

7. Fill in all blanks on federal applications completely. Write N/A (Not Applicable) if appropriate.

8. When responding to a specific request for a proposal (RFP), follow the suggested format as closely as possible.

9. Always include "donated" and "requested" columns in your budget.

10. If appropriate, quote enabling legislation, or foundation founder's words, or a foundation's or corporation's annual report, to show how your project fits the intent of the grant making organization.

11. Make sure you say why this funder is the best source of money for this project.

12. Always include your plan for funding your project after the grant ends.

13. In your summary, emphasize client benefits of your work, and why the project should be funded now.

14. Include copies of endorsement letters and letters from satisfied clients in the appendices of your proposal.

STYLE

1. Use a title that suggests the results you hope to achieve rather than what you plan to do. ("Improving Reading of 5th Graders in Trenton" is better than "A Proposal for Reading Machines for Trenton Schools.")

2. Have a strong first sentence.

3. Use quick openers - like good newspaper openers. Catch the reader's attention early, and keep it.

4. Use short paragraphs (4-6 lines if possible).

5. Don't be afraid to be humorous in a low-key way.

6. Use metaphors, analogies, parables.

7. Write in the third person. It's easier to brag about "they" than "I".

8. Use contractions.

9. Use emotional words (describe love, friendship, grief, etc.)

10. Use the singular form of personal pronouns.

11. Use simple words, but don't insult the reader's intelligence.

12. Use active, not passive voice ("ACT will build the theater in 1982" is better than "The theater will be completed in 1982").

13. Tell a story about people.

14. Aim your "pitch" as though you were writing to one individual.

15. Let a client or expert state your need through a quotation. This lends more credibility than if you state it yourself.

16. When possible, state the need in terms of one person.

17. Beware of "ify" and "hopeful" statements. Be positive.

18. Move from a specific case to a general problem.

19. Accentuate the positive.

   • Emphasize "opportunities," rather than "needs."
   • Funders would rather know "where it's at" than "where it isn't."

20. Mention the amount of money you're requesting at the beginning of your proposal.

21. Have a strong ending.

PROPOSAL EVALUATION FORM

You can use this form in three ways:

1) To review your own proposals, and record suggestions for improvements.

2) In a group, to get everyone's feedback on a particular proposal.

3) Through the mail -- to get people's reaction to a grant proposal you're thinking of submitting.

The Proposal Evaluation Form allows you to quickly critique a proposal, then give constructive positive suggestions for improvement.

PROPOSAL EVALUATION FORM

#	Evaluation Area	Rating: A=good B=accept- able C=poor	Comments and suggested improvements
1.	Title		
2.	Writing style (readability)		
3.	Appropriate tone		
4.	Summary (succinct & motivating)		
5.	Documentation of need		
6.	Establishment of track record		
7.	Explanation of method		
8.	Objectives (specific/ measurable)		
9.	Staff credential/ organization resources		

© 1980 Public Management Institute   (Cont'd.)

PROPOSAL EVALUATION FORM (Cont'd.)

#	Evaluation Area	Rating: A-good B=accept- able C=poor	Comments and suggested improvements
10.	Evaluation design		
11.	Future funding plans		
12.	Budget (thorough)		
13.	Budget (clear)		
14.	Budget (all items justified)		
15.	Appendices		
16.	Logical flow between parts of proposal		
17.	Visual attractiveness		

Omissions/Unnecessary Inclusions in this proposal	Things that should have been emphasized more in this proposal:

© 1980 Public Management Institute

QUESTIONS REVIEWERS ASK: A RATING WORKSHEET

During a proposal review, the five basic areas under consideration are:

1. Scope of Work

2. Personnel

3. Facilities

4. Track Record

5. Budget Information

Various questions will be asked in each area to determine the value of the proposal. The worksheet on the next page has been adapted from an HEW memo of questions in these five areas which was sent to all proposal reviewers. No proposal will be given such comprehensive scrutiny, yet you should prepare as though it were the norm.

The principle of the worksheet is: review yourself before they review you. It helps you understand what agencies want and helps you decide what changes you need to make in your proposal.

This worksheet has been designed with an evaluation system for every question. Be sure you cover each of the five sub-areas in your proposal.

QUESTIONS REVIEWERS ASK: A RATING WORKSHEET

#	Scope of Work-Questions	Need More	Need Less	Accept-able	Suggestions for Improvement
1.	Does the proposal show sufficient understanding of funder priorities and guidelines?				
2.	Do the proposal's objectives fit those of the funder?				
3.	Can the proposal's approach meet its objectives?				
4.	Why is the proposal's approach a good one?				
5.	Has the proposal introduced any elements which could result in delay or expansion of the project?				
6.	Does the proposal have an efficient time schedule?				
7.	Is the time schedule realistic?				
8.	Will proposal reports be issued to coincide with major milestones of the project?				

© 1980 Public Management Institute

(Cont'd.)

#	Scope of Work-Questions	Need More	Need Less	Accept-able	Suggestions for Improvement
9.	Does the proposal provide for the use of community resources and input?				
10.	If a survey sample is needed, has the proposal chosen an adequate one?				
11.	Does the proposal clearly indicate its possible products? (e.g. publications)				
12.	Does the proposal deal with all clearance requirements from federal agencies (e.g., use of animal subjects)?				
13.	Has the proposal set up an efficient and realistic evaluation procedure?				

#	Personnel Questions	Need More	Need Less	Accept-able	Suggestions for Improvement
1.	Does the proposal clearly specify personnel assignments?				
2.	Are personnel assignments time efficient?				

© 1980 Public Management Institute

(Cont'd.)

QUESTIONS REVIEWERS ASK: A RATING WORKSHEET (Cont'd.)

#	Personnel-Questions	Need More	Need Less	Accept-able	Suggestions for Improvement
3.	Are the personnel assigned to specific tasks qualified to perform them (according to experience and training)?				
4.	Is there sufficient information (e.g., vitae) with which to evaluate personnel and their tasks?				
5.	Are the personnel clearly available?				
6.	Have provisions been made to deal with sudden personnel changes?				
7.	Is there efficient administrative management?				
8.	Will there be consultants?				
9.	How will the consultants be used?				
10.	Is the proposal writer one of the key personnel?				
11.	Does the project depend on too many outside personnel?				

© 1980 Public Management Institute

(Cont'd.)

#	Facilities-Questions	Need More	Need Less	Accept-able	Suggestions for Improvement
1.	Has the proposal specified the necessary facilities and equipment?				
2.	Does the proposal make clear its access to outside facilities?				
3.	Are the organizations providing the outside facilities qualified?				
4.	Is the use of facilities realistic in terms of evaluation?				
5.	Is the time schedule realistic for use of outside facilities?				

#	Track Record-Questions	Need More	Need Less	Accept-able	Suggestions for Improvement
1.	Is the organization's track record related to the proposal in a clear way?				
2.	What is the organization's reputation in its field?				
3.	What are the professional honors won by the organization?				

© 1980 Public Management Institute

(Cont'd.)

#	Budget Information-Questions	Need More	Need Less	Accept-able	Suggestions for Improvement
1.	Is the overall proposal budget within the scope of agency funding?				
2.	Are equipment costs clearly stated?				
3.	Is the personnel budget realistic?				
4.	Does the budget account (at a reasonable rate) for use of consultants?				
5.	Does the budget account for use of outside facilities?				
6.	Does the budget cover development of new measuring instruments (e.g., questionnaires for surveys)				

© 1980 Public Management Institute

CONCLUSION

The forms and worksheets provided in this workbook can save you valuable time whenever you write another proposal, or create a new project needing funding.

The completion of **The Quick Proposal Workbook** results in not only a single proposal, but also in the creation of an integral part of an organizational system of grantsmanship.

The final proposal is only a part of the complete grantsmanship process, as described in the preface of this workbook. Preparation for proposal writing should include:

- the creation and implementation of a Grants Readiness System, which insures that all information about your project is organized and easily accessible;

- the establishment of "webbing" networks, with funders and other organizations in your field;

- the development of grant-winning ideas;

- the cross-indexing of these ideas

- the examination of possible budget strategies

- thorough research of potential funders to determine your most likely grant prospects;

- the effective management of your initial contact with funders; and

- the review of information and development of proposal strategies.

Once the proposal is written and reviewed you still need to:

- deal effectively with the funders' decision; and

- develop continued grant support.

The Quick Proposal Workbook has been designed to assist you in:

- developing grant-winning ideas;

- reviewing your information;

- determining proposal strategies;

- writing an individual, tailored proposal;

- revising and evaluating your proposal.

The Public Management Institute would be very happy to receive your suggestions for future editions of The Quick Proposal Workbook. Please contact us:

PUBLIC MANAGEMENT INSTITUTE
358 Brannan Street
San Francisco, CA 94107

Phone: 415/896-1900